The Ship of Death

THE SHIP OF DEATH

Last Poems

D. H. LAWRENCE

Foreword by Frances Wilson

BERGAMOT

The Ship of Death: Last Poems by D. H. Lawrence

www.bergamotbooks.com
Publisher Gail Spilsbury

Publisher's note: *The Ship of Death: Last Poems* presents sixty-seven poems written by D. H. Lawrence shortly before his death in 1930, and first published by Viking Press, New York, in 1933, along with other poems. This volume shares Lawrence's unpublished poems found in manuscript form after his death, except for "The Ship of Death," "Bavarian Gentians," and "Song of Death."

Designed by Jeremy Eberts

Cover: Jo Davidson (American, 1883–1952), *D. H. Lawrence,* 1930, painted terracotta, Metropolitan Museum of Art, New York; photograph courtesy of the University of Nottingham Manuscripts and Special Collections, La Phot 1/35/1

Back cover and frontispiece artwork: Nathan Dickersin-Prokopp

ISBN 979-8-9990175-0-5

PRINTED IN THE UNITED STATES

What we want is to destroy our false, inorganic connections . . . and reestablish the living organic connections, with the cosmos, the sun and earth, with mankind and nation and family. Start with the sun, and the rest will slowly, slowly happen.

D. H. LAWRENCE, *Apocalypse,* 1931

Contents

Foreword

D. H. LAWRENCE died aged forty-four in March 1930, and these sixty-seven poems, a song-cycle celebrating his love of being alive and philosophy of renewal, were his preparation for the "sweet dark oblivion" he had long refused to acknowledge. Until the very end, Lawrence explained to friends that his tuberculosis, contracted as a young man, was a bronchial condition from which he would soon recover. It was typical of him to both accept and deny that he was dying: a deeply religious atheist, Lawrence was built of contradictions.

Few things move me more than the fading out of Lawrence's exhausting, exhilarating life, or the account that he leaves in "The Ship of Death," the centrepiece to this book of bidding "farewell / to one's own self." He described death as "the longest journey," but his journey from the Nottingham miner's cottage where he was born to the hilltop town of Vence, France, where he died, feels equally long. Lawrence lived hard and wild, and mostly on the run. He fled, as though pursued, between England, Italy, Sicily, Ceylon, Australia, New Mexico, and Mexico, until pausing for breath in the bungalow on the Côte d'Azur, where we can imagine him now sitting up in bed writing these lines, his notebook resting on his knees, his pencil moving swiftly and neatly across each page.

Writing came to Lawrence spontaneously; he describes the process in "The Work of Creation," my favorite of his last poems, as "a great strange urge," which has nothing to do with the "mind." Because he was a time traveler, when he looked through his bedroom window at the Mediterranean Sea, which lay fifty yards from the garden, he saw the "ships of Cnossos," as he says in his opening poem "The Greeks Are Coming!" and "men with archaic pointed beards." He also saw his own "little ship, with oars and food / and little dishes, and all accoutrements / fitting and ready for the departing soul," in "The Ship of Death." Lawrence never felt more connected to the universe than on a ship, so it was in keeping that he imagined death as an eternal voyage in an "ark of faith." A mystic rather than a modernist, Lawrence loathed modernity with its jazz and films and poison gas, and he rightly feared for the future. The world he was escaping on his "fragile ship of courage" included the ugly "ocean liner" he also saw from his bedroom window, trailing its "long thread of dark smoke / like a bad smell."

These poems, some of which are revisions of one another or second attempts at the same idea, record Lawrence's consciousness in full flow, and catch his famously mercurial temperament. He moves between rage at "the evil world-soul of to-day," reverie at the elegance of the ancient world, joy at the redness of a geranium, and childlike wonder at natural phenomena such as rainbows and the mating of whales. In "Whales Weep Not!", a poem only Lawrence could have written, he imagines two of the earth's largest mammals rocking "with love" and rolling "with massive, strong desire, like gods." Lawrence, who weighed eighty-five pounds when he wrote these lines, knew that Frieda, his buxom, promiscuous wife, was already sleeping with the handsome Italian army officer who would become her next husband. He had a slow and dreadful death, but we will not find in Lawrence a drop of self-pity.

"We buried him, very simply," Frieda wrote, "like a bird we put him away." And like the phoenix in his magnificent final poem, he rose a figure of myth from the "hot and flocculent ash."

FRANCES WILSON
Author of *Burning Man: The Trials of D. H. Lawrence*

The Ship of Death

The Greeks Are Coming!

Little islands out at sea, on the horizon
keep suddenly showing a whiteness, a flash and a furl, a hail
of something coming, ships a-sail from over the rim of the sea.

And every time, it is ships, it is ships
it is ships of Cnossos coming, out of the morning and the sea,
it is Aegean ships, and men with archaic pointed beards
coming out of the Eastern end.

But it is far-off foam.
And an ocean liner, going east, like a small beetle walking the edge
is leaving a long thread of dark smoke
like a bad smell.

The Argonauts

They are not dead, they are not dead!
Now that the sun, like a lion, licks his paws
and goes slowly down the hill:
now that the moon, who remembers, and only cares
that we should be lovely in the flesh, with bright crescent feet,
pauses near the crest of the hill, climbing slowly, like a queen
looking down on the lion as he retreats.

Now the sea is the Argonauts' sea, and in the dawn
Odysseus calls the commands, as he steers past those foamy islands
wait, wait, don't bring the coffee yet, nor the *pain grillé*.
The dawn is not off the sea, and Odysseus' ships
have not yet passed the islands. I must watch them still.

Middle of the World

This sea will never die, neither will it ever grow old
nor cease to be blue, nor in the dawn
cease to lift up its hills
and let the slim black ship of Dionysos come sailing in
with grape-vines up the mast, and dolphins leaping.

What do I care if the smoking ships
of the P. & O. and the Orient Line and all the other stinkers
cross like clock-work the Minoan distance!
They only cross, the distance never changes.

And now that the moon who gives men glistening bodies
is in her exaltation, and can look down on the sun
I see descending from the ships at dawn
slim naked men from Cnossos, smiling the archaic smile
of those that will without fail come back again,
and kindling little fires upon the shores
and crouching, and speaking the music of lost languages.

And the Minoan Gods, and the Gods of Tiryns[1]
are heard softly laughing and chatting, as ever;
and Dionysos, young, and a stranger
leans listening on the gate, in all respect.

For the Heroes Are Dipped in Scarlet

Before Plato told the great lie of ideals
men slimly went like fishes, and didn't care.

They had long hair, like Samson,
and clean as arrows they sped at the mark
when the bow-cord twanged.

They knew it was no use knowing
their own nothingness:
for they were not nothing.

So now they come back! Hark!
Hark! the low and shattering laughter of bearded men
with the slim waists of warriors, and the long feet
of moon-lit dancers.

Oh, and their faces scarlet, like the dolphin's blood!
Lo! the loveliest is red all over, rippling vermilion
as he ripples upwards!
laughing in his black beard!

They are dancing! they return, as they went, dancing!
For the thing that is done without the glowing as of god, vermilion,
were best not done at all.
How glistening red they are!

Demiurge

They say that reality exists only in the spirit
that corporal existence is a kind of death
that pure being is bodiless
that the idea of the form precedes the form substantial.[2]

But what nonsense it is!
as if any Mind could have imagined a lobster
dozing the under-deeps, then reaching out a savage and iron claw!

Even the mind of God can only imagine
those things that have become themselves:
bodies and presences, here and now, creatures with a foothold
    in creation
even if it is only a lobster on tip-toe.

Religion knows better than philosophy
Religion knows that Jesus never was Jesus
till he was born from a womb, and ate soup and bread
and grew up, and became, in the wonder of creation, Jesus,
with a body and with needs, and a lovely spirit.

The Work of Creation

The mystery of creation is the divine urge of creation,
but it is a great strange urge, it is not a Mind.
Even an artist knows that his work was never in his mind,
he could never have *thought* it before it happened.
A strange ache possessed him, and he entered the struggle,
and out of the struggle with his material, in the spell of the urge
his work took place, it came to pass, it stood up and saluted his mind.

God is a great urge, wonderful, mysterious, magnificent
but he knows nothing before-hand.
His urge takes shape in flesh, and lo!
it is creation! God looks himself on it in wonder, for the first time.
Lo! there is a creature, formed! How strange!
Let me think about it! Let me form an idea!

Red Geranium and Godly Mignonette

Imagine that any mind ever *thought* a red geranium!
As if the redness of a red geranium could be anything but a
sensual experience
and as if sensual experience could take place before there were
any senses.
We know that even God could not imagine the redness of a
red geranium
nor the smell of mignonette
when geraniums were not, and mignonette neither.
And even when they were, even God would have to have a nose
to smell at the mignonette.
You can't imagine the Holy Ghost sniffing at cherry-pie heliotrope.
Or the Most High, during the coal age, cudgelling his mighty brains
even if he had any brains: straining his mighty mind
to think, among the moss and mud of lizards and mastodons
to think out, in the abstract, when all was twilit green and muddy:
"Now there shall be tum-tiddly-um, and tum-tiddly-um,
hey-presto! scarlet geranium!"

We know it couldn't be done.

But imagine, among the mud and the mastodons
god sighing and yearning with tremendous creative yearning, in
that dark green mess
oh, for some other beauty, some other beauty
that blossomed at last, red geranium, and mignonette.

Bodiless God

Everything that has beauty has a body, and is a body;
everything that has being has being in the flesh:
and dreams are only drawn from the bodies that are.

And God?
Unless God has a body, how can he have a voice
and emotions, and desires, and strength, glory or honour?
For God, even the rarest God, is supposed to love us
and wish us to be this that and the other.
And he is supposed to be mighty and glorious.

The Body of God

God is the great urge that has not yet found a body
but urges towards incarnation with the great creative urge.

And becomes at last a clove carnation:[3] lo! that is god!
and becomes at last Helen, or Ninon:[4] any lovely and generous
    woman
at her best and her most beautiful, being god, made manifest,
any clear and fearless man being god, very god.

There is no god
apart from poppies and the flying fish,
men singing songs, and women brushing their hair in the sun.
The lovely things are god that has come to pass, like Jesus came.
The rest, the undiscoverable, is the demiurge.

The Rainbow

Even the rainbow has a body
made of the drizzling rain
and is an architecture of glistening atoms
built up, built up
yet you can't lay your hand on it,
nay, nor even your mind.

Maximus

God is older than the sun and moon
and the eye cannot behold him
nor voice describe him.

But a naked man, a stranger, leaned on the gate
with his cloak over his arm, waiting to be asked in.
So I called him: Come in, if you will!—
He came in slowly, and sat down by the hearth.
I said to him: And what is your name?—
He looked at me without answer, but such a loveliness
entered me, I smiled to myself, saying: He is God!
So he said: *Hermes!*
God is older than the sun and moon
and the eye cannot behold him
nor the voice describe him:
and still, this is the God Hermes, sitting by my hearth.

The Man of Tyre

The man of Tyre[5] went down to the sea
pondering, for he was Greek, that God is one and all alone and
ever more shall be so.

And a woman who had been washing clothes in the pool of rock
where a stream came down to the gravel of the sea and sank in,
who had spread white washing on the gravel banked above the bay,
who had lain her shift on the shore, on the shingle slope,
who had waded to the pale green sea of evening, out to a shoal,
pouring sea-water over herself
now turned, and came slowly back, with her back to the evening sky.

Oh lovely, lovely with the dark hair piled up, as she went deeper,
deeper down the channel, then rose shallower, shallower,
with the full thighs slowly lifting of the wader wading shorewards
and the shoulders pallid with light from the silent sky behind
both breasts dim and mysterious, with the glamorous kindness
of twilight between them
and the dim blotch of black maidenhair like an indicator,
giving a message to the man—

So in the cane-brake[6] he clasped his hands in delight
that could only be god-given, and murmured:
Lo! God is one god! But here in the twilight
godly and lovely comes Aphrodite out of the sea
towards me!

They Say the Sea Is Loveless

They say the sea is loveless, that in the sea
love cannot live, but only bare, salt splinters
of loveless life.
But from the sea
the dolphins leap round Dionysos' ship
whose masts have purple vines,
and up they come with the purple dark of rainbows
and flip! they go! with the nose-dive of sheer delight;
and the sea is making love to Dionysos
in the bouncing of these small and happy whales.

Whales Weep Not!

They say the sea is cold, but the sea contains
the hottest blood of all, and the wildest, the most urgent.

All the whales in the wider deeps, hot are they, as they urge
on and on, and dive beneath the ice-bergs.
The right whales, the sperm-whales, the hammer-heads, the killers
there they blow, there they blow, hot wild white breath out of
the sea!

And they rock and they rock, through the sensual ageless ages
on the depths of the seven seas,
and through the salt they reel with drunk delight
and in the tropics tremble they with love
and roll with massive, strong desire, like gods.
Then the great bull lies up against his bride
in the blue deep of the sea
as mountain pressing on mountain, in the zest of life:
and out of the inward roaring of the inner red ocean of whale blood
the long tip reaches strong, intense, like the maelstrom-tip, and
comes to rest
in the clasp and the soft, wild clutch of a she-whale's fathomless body.

And over the bridge of the whale's strong phallus, linking the
wonder of whales
the burning archangels under the sea keep passing, back and forth,
keep passing archangels of bliss
from him to her, from her to him, great Cherubim
that wait on whales in mid-ocean, suspended in the waves of the sea

great heaven of whales in the waters, old hierarchies.
And enormous mother whales lie dreaming suckling their whale-
tender young
and dreaming with strange whale eyes wide open in the waters of
the beginning and the end.

And bull-whales gather their women and whale-calves in a ring
when danger threatens, on the surface of the ceaseless flood
and range themselves like great fierce Seraphim facing the threat
encircling their huddled monsters of love.
And all this happiness in the sea, in the salt
where God is also love, but without words:
and Aphrodite is the wife of whales
most happy, happy she!

And Venus among the fishes skips and is a she-dolphin
she is the gay, delighted porpoise sporting with love and the sea
she is the female tunny-fish, round and happy among the males
and dense with happy blood, dark rainbow bliss in the sea.

Invocation to the Moon

You beauty, O you beauty
you glistening, garmentless beauty!
great lady, great glorious lady
greatest of ladies
crownless and jewelless and garmentless
because naked you are more wonderful than anything we can stroke.

Be good to me, lady, great lady of the nearest
heavenly mansion, and last!
Now I am at your gate, you beauty, you lady of all nakedness!
Now I must enter your mansion, and beg your gift
Moon, O Moon, great lady of the heavenly few.

Far and forgotten is the Villa of Venus the glowing
and behind me now in the gulfs of space lies the golden house
    of the sun,
and six have given me gifts, and kissed me god-speed
kisses of four great lords, beautiful, as they held me to their
    bosom in farewell,
and kiss of the far-off lingering lady who looks over the distant
    fence of the twilight,
and one warm kind kiss of the lion with golden paws.

Now, lady of the Moon, now open the gate of your silvery house
and let me come past the silver bells of your flowers and the
    cockleshells

into your house, garmentless lady of the last great gift:
who will give me back my lost limbs
and my lost white fearless breast
and set me again on moon-remembering feet
a healed, whole man, O Moon!

Lady, lady of the last house down the long, long street of the stars
be good to me now, as I beg you, as you've always been good to men
who begged of you and gave you homage
and watched for your glistening feet down the garden path!

Butterfly

Butterfly, the wind blows sea-ward, strong beyond the garden wall!
Butterfly, why do you settle on my shoe, and sip the dirt on my shoe,
lifting your veined wings, lifting them? big white butterfly!

Already it is October, and the wind blows strong to the sea
from the hills where the snow must have fallen, the wind is polished
with snow.
Here in the garden, with red geraniums, it is warm, it is warm
but the wind blows strong to sea-ward, white butterfly, content on
my shoe!

Will you go, will you go from my warm house?
Will you climb on your big soft wings, black-dotted,
as up an invisible rainbow, an arch
till the wind slides you sheer from the arch-crest
and in a strange level fluttering you go out to sea-ward, white speck!

Farewell, farewell, lost soul!
you have melted in the crystalline distance,
it is enough! I saw you vanish into air.

Bavarian Gentians

Not every man has gentians[7] in his house
in Soft September at slow, sad Michaelmas.[8]

Bavarian gentians, big and dark, only dark
darkening the day-time torch-like with the smoking blueness of
    Pluto's gloom,
ribbed and torch-like, with their blaze of darkness spread blue
down flattening into points, flattened under the sweep of white day
torch-flower of the blue-smoking darkness, Pluto's dark-blue daze,
black lamps from the halls of Dio, burning dark blue,
giving off darkness, blue darkness, as Demeter's pale lamps give
    off light,
lead me then, lead me the way.

Reach me a gentian, give me a torch!
let me guide myself with the blue, forked torch of this flower
down the darker and darker stairs, where blue is darkened on
    blueness
even where Persephone goes, just now, from the frosted September
to the sightless realm where darkness is awake upon the dark
and Persephone herself is but a voice
or a darkness invisible enfolded in the deeper dark
of the arms Plutonic, and pierced with the passion of dense gloom,
among the splendor of torches of darkness, shedding darkness on
    the lost bride and her groom.

Lucifer

Angels are bright still, though the brightest fell.
But tell me, tell me, how do you know
he lost any of his brightness in the falling?
In the dark-blue depths, under layers and layers of darkness
I see him more like the ruby, a gleam from within
of his own magnificence
coming like the ruby in the invisible dark, glowing
with his own annunciation, towards us.

The Breath of Life

The breath of life is in the sharp winds of change
mingled with the breath of destruction.
But if you want to breathe deep, sumptuous life
breathe all alone, in silence, in the dark,
and see nothing.

Silence

Come, holy Silence, come
great bride of all creation.
Come, holy Silence! reach, reach
from the presence of God, and envelope us.

Let the sea heave no more in sound,
hold the stars still, lest we hear the heavens dimly ring with their commotion!
fold up all sounds.

Lo! the laugh of God!
Lo! the laugh of the creator!
Lo! the last of the seven great laughs of God!
Lo! the last of the seven great laughs of creation!

Huge, huge roll the peals of the thundrous laugh
huge, huger, huger and huger pealing
till they mount and fill and all is fulfilled of God's last and greatest laugh
till all is soundless and senseless, a tremendous body of silence
enveloping even the edges of the thought-waves
enveloping even me, who hear no more,
who am embedded in a shell of silence,
of silence, lovely silence
of endless and living silence
of holy silence
the silence of the last of the seven great laughs of God.
Ah! the holy silence—it is meet!
It is very fitting! there is nought beside!

For now we are passing through the gate, stilly,
in the sacred silence of gates
in the silence of passing through doors,
in the great hush of going for this into that,
in the suspension of wholeness, in the moment of division within
the whole!

Lift up your heads, O ye Gates!
for the silence of the last great thunderous laugh
screens us purely, and we can slip through.

The Hands of God

It is a fearful thing to fall into the hands of the living God.
But it is a much more fearful thing to fall out of them.

Did Lucifer fall through knowledge?
oh then, pity him, pity him that plunge!

Save me, O God, from falling into the ungodly knowledge
of myself as I am without God.
Let me never know, O God
let me never know what I am or should be
when I have fallen out of your hands, the hands of the living God.

That awful and sickening endless sinking, sinking
through the slow, corruptive levels of disintegrative knowledge
when the self has fallen from the hands of God
and sinks, seething and sinking, corrupt
and sinking still, in depth after depth of disintegrative
    consciousness
sinking in the endless undoing, the awful katabolism[9] into the abyss!
even of the soul, fallen from the hands of God!

Save me from that, O God!
Let me never know myself apart from the living God!

Pax

All that matters is to be at one with the living God
to be a creature in the house of the God of Life.

Like a cat asleep on a chair
at peace, in peace
and at one with the master of the house, with the mistress,
at home, at home in the house of the living,
sleeping on the hearth, and yawning before the fire.

Sleeping on the hearth of the living world
yawning at home before the fire of life
feeling the presence of the living God
like a great reassurance
a deep calm in the heart
a presence
as of the master sitting at the board
in his own and great being,
in the house of life.

Abysmal Immortality

It is not easy to fall out of the hands of the living God
They are so large, and they cradle so much of a man.
It is a long time before a man can get himself away.
Even through the greatest blasphemies, the hands of the living
    God still continue to cradle him.

And still through knowledge and will, he can break away
man can break away, and fall from the hands of God
into himself alone, down the godless plunge of the abyss,
a god-lost creature turning upon himself
in the long, long fall, revolving upon himself
in the endless writhe of the last, the last self-knowledge
which he can never reach till he touch the bottom of the abyss
which he can never touch, for the abyss is bottomless.

And there is nothing else, throughout time and eternity
but the abyss, which is bottomless,
and the fall to extinction, which can never come,
for the abyss is bottomless,
and the turning down plunge of writhing of self-knowledge,
    self-analysis
which goes further and further, and yet never finds an end
for there is no end,
it is the abyss of the immortality
of those that have fallen from God.

Only Man

Only man can fall from God
Only man.

No animal, no beast nor creeping thing
no cobra nor hyaena nor scorpion nor hideous white ant
can slip entirely through the fingers of the hands of God
into the abyss of self-knowledge,
knowledge of the self-apart-from-God.

For the knowledge of the self-apart-from-God
is an abyss down which the soul can slip
writhing and twisting in all revolutions
of the unfinished plunge
of self-awareness, now apart from God, falling
fathomless, fathomless, self-consciousness wriggling
writhing deeper and deeper in all the minutiae of self-knowledge,
downwards, exhaustive,
yet never, never coming to the bottom, for there is no bottom,
zigzagging down like the fizzle from a finished rocket
the frizzling falling fire that cannot go out, dropping wearily,
neither can it reach the depth
for the depth is bottomless,
so it wriggles its way even further down, further down
at last in sheer horror of not being able to leave off
knowing itself, knowing itself apart from God, falling.

Return of Returns

Come in a week
Yes, yes, in the seven-day-week!
for how can I count in your three times three
of the sea-blown week of nine.

Come then, as I say, in a week,
when the planets have given seven nods
"It shall be! It shall be!" assented seven times
by the great seven, by Helios the brightest
and by Artemis the whitest
by Hermes and Aphrodite, flashing white glittering words,
by Ares and Kronos and Zeus,
the seven great ones, who must all say yes.

When the moon from out of the darkness
has come like a thread, like a door just opening
opening, till the round white doorway of delight
is half open.

Come then!
Then, when the door is half open.
In a week!
The ancient river week, the old one.
Come then!

Stoic

Groan then, groan,
For the sun is dead, and all that is in heaven
is the pyre of blazing gas.

And the moon that went
so queenly, shaking her glistening beams
is dead too, a dead orb wheeled once a month round the park.

And the five others, the travellers
they are all dead!
In the hearse of night you see their tarnished coffins
travelling, travelling still, still travelling
to the end, for they are not yet buried.

Groan then, groan!
Groan then, for even the maiden earth
is dead, we run wheels across her corpse.

Oh groan
groan with mighty groans!

But for all that, and all that
"in the centre of your being, groan not."
In the centre of your being, groan not, do not groan.
For perhaps the greatest of all illusions
is this illusion of the death of the undying.

In the Cities

In the cities
there is even no more any weather
the weather in town is always benzine, or else petrol fumes
lubricating oil, exhaust gas.

As over some dense marsh, the fumes
thicken, miasma, the fumes of the automobile
densely thicken in the cities.

In ancient Rome, down the thronged streets
no wheels might run, no insolent chariots.
Only the footsteps, footsteps
of people
and the gentle trotting of the litter-bearers.

In Minos, in Mycenae
in all the cities with lion gates
the dead threaded the air, lingering
lingering in the earth's shadow
and leaning towards the old hearth.

In London, New York, Paris
in the bursten cities
the dead tread heavily through the muddy air
through the mire of fumes
heavily, stepping weary on our hearts.

Lord's Prayer

For thine is the kingdom
the power, and the glory.

Hallowed by thy name, then
Thou who are nameless.

Give me, Oh give me
besides my daily bread
my kingdom, my power, and my glory.

All things that turn to thee
have their kingdom, their power, and their glory.
Like the kingdom of the nightingale at twilight
whose power and glory I have often heard and felt.

Like the kingdom of the fox in the dark
yapping in his power and his glory
which is death to the goose.

Like the power and the glory of the goose in the mist
hawking over the lake.

And I, a naked man, calling
calling to thee for my mana,[10]
my kingdom, my power, and my glory.

Mana of the Sea

Do you see the sea, breaking itself to bits against the islands
yet remaining unbroken, the level great sea?

Have I caught from it
the tide in my arms
that runs down to the shallows of my wrists, and breaks
abroad in my hands, like waves among the rocks of substance?

Do the rollers of the sea
roll down my thighs
and over the submerged islets of my knees
with power, sea-power
sea-power
to break against the ground
in the flat, recurrent breakers of my two feet?

And is my body ocean, ocean
whose power runs to the shores along my arms
and breaks in the foamy hands, whose power rolls out
to the white-treading waves of two salt feet?

I am the sea! I am the sea!

Salt

Salt is scorched water that the sun has scorched
into substance and flaky whiteness
in the eternal opposition
between the two great ones, Fire, and the Wet.

The Four

To our senses, the elements are four
and have ever been, and will ever be
for they are the elements of life, of poetry, and of perception
the four Great Ones, the Four Roots, the First Four
of Fire and the Wet, Earth and the wide Air of the world.

To find the other many elements, you must go to the laboratory
and hunt them down.
But the four we have always with us, they are our world.
Or rather, they have us with them.

The Boundary Stone

So, salt is the boundary mark between Fire that burns, and the Wet.
It is the white stone of limits, the term, the landmark between
the two great and moving Ones, Fire and the yielding Wet.
It is set up as a boundary, and blood and sweat
are marked out with the boundary of salt, between Fire and the Wet.

Spilling the Salt

Don't spill the salt, for it is the landmark,
and cursed be he that removeth his neighbour's landmark.

And the watchers, the dividers, those swift ones with dark
    sharp wings
and keen eyes, they will hover, they will come between you,
between you and your purpose like a knife's edge shadow
cutting you off from your joy.

For the unseen witnesses are the angels of creation
but also the sunderers, the angels with black, sharp wing-tips.

Walk Warily

Walk warily, walk warily, be careful what you say:
because now the Sunderers are hovering round,
the Dividers are close upon us, dogging our every breath
and watching our every step,
and beating their great wings in our panting faces.

The angels are standing back, the angels of the Kiss.
They wait, they give way now
to the Sunderers, to the swift ones
the ones with the sharp black wings
and the shudder of electric anger
and the drumming of pinions of thunder
and hands like salt
and the sudden dripping down of the knife-edge cleavage of
 the lightning
cleaving, cleaving.

Lo, we are in the midst of the sunderers
the cleavers, that cleave us forever apart from one another,
and separate heart from heart, and cut away all caresses
with the white triumphance of lightning and electric delight,
the Dividers, the Thunderers, the Swift Ones, blind with speed
who put salt in our mouths
and currents of excitement in our limbs
and hotness, and then more crusted brine in our hearts.

It is the day of the Sunderers
and the angels are standing back.

Mystic

They call all experiences of the senses *mystic,* when the experience is considered.
So an apple becomes *mystic* when I taste in it
the summer and the snows, the wild welter of earth
and the insistence of the sun.
All of which things I can surely taste in a good apple.
Though some apples taste preponderantly of water, wet and sour
and some of too much sun, brackish sweet
like lagoon-water, that has been too much sunned.
If I say I taste these things in an apple, I am called *mystic,* which means a liar.
The only way to eat an apple is to hog it down like a pig
and taste nothing
that is *real.*

But if I eat an apple, I like to eat it with all my senses awake.
Hogging it down like a pig I call the feeding of corpses.

Anaxagoras

When Anaxagoras[11] says: Even the snow is black!
he is taken by scientists very seriously
because he is enunciating a "principle," a "law"
that all things are mixed, and therefore the purest white snow
has in it an element of blackness.

That they call science, and reality.
I call it mental conceit and mystification
and nonsense, for pure snow is white to us
white and white and only white
with a lovely bloom of whiteness upon white
in which the soul delights and the senses
have an experience of bliss.

And life is for delight, and for bliss
and dread, and the dark, rolling ominousness of doom
then the bright dawning of delight again
from off the sheer white snow, or the poised moon.

And in the shadow of the sun the snow is blue, so blue-aloof
with a hint of the frozen bells of the scylla flower
but never the ghost of a glimpse of Anaxagoras' funeral black.

Kissing and Horrid Strife

I have been defeated and dragged down by pain
and worsted by the evil world-soul of to-day.

But still I know that life is for delight
and for bliss
as now when the tiny wavelets of the sea
tip the morning light on edge, and spill it with delight
to show how inexhaustible it is.

And life is for delight, and bliss
like now where the white sun kisses the sea
and plays with the wavelets like a panther playing with its cubs
cuffing them with soft paws,
and blows that are caresses,
kisses of the soft-balled paws, where the talons are.

And life is for dread,
for doom that darkens, and the Sunderers
that sunder us from each other
that strip us and destroy us and break us down
as the tall fox-gloves and the mulleins and mallows
are torn down by dismembering autumn
till not a vestige is left, and bleak winter has no trace
of any such flowers;
and yet the roots below the blackness are intact:
the Thunderers and the Sunderers have their term
their limit, their thus far and no further.

Life is for kissing and for horrid strife.
Life is for the angels and the Sunderers
Life is for the daimons and the demons
those that put honey on our lips, and those that put salt.

But life is not
for the dead vanity of knowing better, nor the blank
cold superiority, nor silly
conceit of being immune,
nor puerility of contradictions
like saying snow is black, or desire is evil.

Life is for kissing and for horrid strife,
the angels and the Sunderers.
And perhaps in unknown Death we perhaps shall know
Oneness and poised immunity.
But why then should we die while we can live?
And while we live
the kissing and communing cannot cease
nor yet the striving and the horrid strife.

When Satan Fell

When Satan fell, he only fell
because the Lord Almighty rose a bit too high,
a bit beyond himself.

So Satan only fell to keep a balance.
"Are you so lofty, O my God?
Are you so pure and lofty, up aloft?
Then I will fall, and plant the paths to hell
with vines and poppies and fig-trees
so that lost souls may eat grapes
and the moist fig
and put scarlet buds in their hair on the way to hell,
on the way to the dark perdition."

And hell and heaven are the scales of the balance of life
which swing against each other.

Doors

But evil is a third thing,
No, not the ithyphallic[12] demons
not even the double Phallus of the devil himself
with his key to the two dark doors
is evil.

Life has its palace of blue day aloft
and its halls of the great dark below,
and there are the bright doors where souls go gaily in:
and there are the dark doors where souls pass silently
holding their breath, naked and darkly alone
entering into the other communion.

There is a double sacredness of doors.
Some you may sing through, and all men hear,
but others, the dark doors, oh hush! hush!
let nobody be about! slip in! go all unseen.
But evil, evil is another thing! in another place!

Evil Is Homeless

Evil has no home,
only evil has no home,
not even the home of demoniacal hell.
Hell is the home of souls lost in darkness,
even as heaven is the home of souls lost in light.
And like Persephone, or Attis[13]
there are souls that are at home in both homes.
Not like grey Dante, colour-blind
to the scarlet and purple flowers at the doors of hell.

But evil
evil has no dwelling-place
the grey vulture, the grey hyaena, corpse-eaters
they dwell in the outskirt fringes of nowhere
where the grey twilight of evil sets in.

And men that sit in machines
among spinning wheels, in an apotheosis of wheels
sit in the grey mist of movement which moves not
and going which goes not
and doing which does not
and being which is not:
that is, they sit and are evil, in evil,
grey evil, which has no path, and shows neither light nor dark
and has no home, no home anywhere.

What Then Is Evil?

Oh, in the world of the flesh of man
iron gives the deadly wound
and the wheel starts the principle of all evil.

Oh, in the world of things
the wheel is the first principle of evil.

But in the world of the soul of man
there, and there alone lies the pivot of pure evil
only in the soul of man, when it pivots upon the ego.

When the mind makes a wheel which turns on the hub of the ego
and the will, the living dynamo, gives the motion and the speed
and the wheel of the conscious self spins on in absolution, absolute
absolute, absolved from the sun and the earth and the moon,
absolute consciousness, absolved from strife and kisses
absolute self-awareness, absolved from the meddling of creation
absolute freedom, absolved from the great necessities of being
then we see evil, pure evil
and we see it only in man
and in his machines.

The Evil World-Soul

Oh, there is evil, there is an evil world-soul.
But it is the soul of man only, and his machines
which has brought to pass the fearful thing called evil.
Hyaenas only hint at it.

Do not think that a machine is without a soul.
Every wheel on its hub has a soul, evil,
it is part of the evil world-soul, spinning.

And every man who has become a detached and self-activated ego
is evil, evil, part of the evil world-soul
which wishes to blaspheme the world into greyness,
into evil neutrality, into mechanism.
The Robot is the unit of evil.
And the symbol of the Robot is the wheel revolving.

The Wandering Cosmos

Oh, do not tell me the heavens as well are a wheel.
For every revolution of the earth around the sun
is a footstep onwards, onwards, we know not whither
and we do not care,
but a step onwards in untravelled space,
for the earth, like the sun, is a wanderer.
Their going round each time is a step
onwards, we know not whither,
but onwards, onwards, for the heavens are wandering
the moon and the earth, the sun, Saturn and Betelgeuse,
    Vega and Sirius and Altair
they wander their strange and different ways in heaven
past Venus and Uranus and the signs.

For life is a wandering, we know not whither, but going.

Only the wheel goes round, but it never wanders.
It stays on its hub.

Death Is Not Evil, Evil Is Mechanical

Only the human being, absolved from kissing and strife
goes on and on and on, without wandering
fixed upon the hub of the ego
going, yet never wandering, fixed, yet in motion,
the kind of hell that is real, grey and awful
sinless and stainless going round and round
the kind of hell grey Dante never saw
but of which he had a bit inside him.

Know thyself, and that thou art mortal.
But know thyself, denying that thou art mortal:
a thing of kisses and strife
a lit-up shaft of rain
a calling column of blood
a rose tree bronzey with thorns
a mixture of yea and nay
a rainbow of love and hate
a wind that blows back and forth
a creature of conflict, like a cataract:
know thyself, in denial of all these things.

And thou shalt begin to spin round on the hub of the obscene ego
a grey void thing that goes without wandering
a machine that in itself is nothing
a centre of the evil-world.

Strife

When strife is a thing of two
each knows the other in struggle
and the conflict is a communion
of twoness.

But when strife is a thing of one
a single ego striving for its own ends
and beating down resistances
then strife is evil, because it is not strife.

The Late War

The War was not strife
it was murder
each side trying to murder the other side
evilly.

Murder

Killing is not evil.
A man may be my enemy to the death,
and that is passion and communion.

But murder is always evil
being an act of one
perpetrated upon the other
without cognisance or communion.

Murderous Weapons

So guns and strong explosives
are evil, evil
they let death upon unseen men
in sheer murder.

And most murderous of all devices
are poison gases and air-bombs
refinement of evil.

Departure

Now some men must get up and depart
from evil, or all is lost.

The evil will in many evil men
makes an evil world-soul, which purposes
to reduce the world to grey ash.
Wheels are evil
and machines are evil
and the will to make money is evil.

All forms of abstraction are evil:
finance is a great evil abstraction
science has now become an evil abstraction
education is an evil abstraction.

Jazz and film and wireless
are all evil abstractions from life.

And politics, now, are an evil abstraction from life.

Evil is upon us and has got hold of us.
Men must depart from it, or all is lost.
We must make an isle impregnable
against evil.

The Ship of Death

Now it is autumn and the falling fruit
and the long journey towards oblivion.

The apples falling like great drops of dew
to bruise themselves an exit from themselves.

And it is time to go, to bid farewell
to one's own self, and find an exit
from the fallen self.

II

Have you built your ship of death, O have you?
O build your ship of death, for you will need it.

The grim frost is at hand, when the apples will fall
thick, almost thundrous, on the hardened earth.

And death is on the air like a smell of ashes!
Ah! can't you smell it?
And in the bruised body, the frightened soul
finds itself shrinking, wincing from the cold
that blows upon it through the orifices.

III

And can a man his own quietus make
with a bare bodkin?

With daggers, bodkins, bullets, man can make
a bruise or break of exit for his life;
but is that a quietus, O tell me, it is quietus?

Surely not so! for how could murder, even self-murder
ever a quietus make?

IV

O let us talk of quiet that we know,
that we can know, the deep and lovely quiet
of a strong heart at peace!

How can we this, our own quietus, make?

V

Build then the ship of death, for you must take
the longest journey, to oblivion.

And die the death, the long and painful death
that lies between the old self and the new.

Already our bodies are fallen, bruised, badly bruised,
already our souls are oozing through the exit
of the cruel bruise.

Already the dark and endless ocean of the end
is washing in through the breaches of our wounds,
already the flood is upon us.

Oh build your ship of death, your little ark
and furnish it with food, with little cakes, and wine
for the dark flight down oblivion.

VI

Piecemeal the body dies, and the timid soul
has her footing washed away, as the dark flood rises.

We are dying, we are dying, we are all of us dying
and nothing will stay the death-flood rising within us
and soon it will rise on the world, on the outside world.

We are dying, we are dying, piecemeal our bodies are dying
and our strength leaves us,
and our soul cowers naked in the dark rain over the flood,
cowering in the last branches of the tree of our life.

VII

We are dying, we are dying, so all we can do
is now to be willing to die, and to build the ship
of death to carry the soul on the longest journey.

A little ship, with oars and food
and little dishes, and all accoutrements
fitting and ready for the departing soul.

Now launch the small ship, now as the body dies
and life departs, launch out, the fragile soul
in the fragile ship of courage, the ark of faith
with its store of food and little cooking pans
and change of clothes,
upon the flood's black waste
upon the waters of the end
upon the sea of death, where still we sail
darkly, for we cannot steer, and have no port.

There is no port, there is nowhere to go
only the deepening blackness, darkening still
blacker upon the soundless, ungurgling flood
darkness at one with darkness, up and down
and sideways utterly dark, so there is no direction any more.
And the little ship is there; yet she is gone.
She is not seen, for there is nothing to see her by.
She is gone! gone! and yet
somewhere she is there.
Nowhere!

VIII

And everything is gone, the body is gone
completely under, gone, entirely gone.
The upper darkness is heavy as the lower,
between them the little ship
is gone

It is the end, it is oblivion

IX

And yet out of eternity a thread
separates itself on the blackness,
a horizontal thread
that fumes a little with pallor upon the dark.

Is it illusion? or does the pallor fume
a little higher?
Ah wait, wait, for there's the dawn,
the cruel dawn of coming back to life
out of oblivion.

Wait, wait, the little ship
drifting, beneath the deathly ashy grey
of a flood-dawn.

Wait, wait! even so, a flush of yellow
and strangely, O chilled wan soul, a flush of rose.

A flush of rose, and the whole thing starts again.

X

The flood subsides, and the body, like a worn sea-shell
emerges strange and lovely.
And the little ship wings home, faltering and lapsing
on the pink flood,
and the frail soul steps out, into the house again
filling the heart with peace.

Swings the heart renewed with peace
even of oblivion.

Oh build your ship of death. Oh build it!
for you will need it.
For the voyage of oblivion awaits you.

Difficult Death

It is not easy to die, O it is not easy
to die the death.

For death comes when he will
not when we will him.

And we can be dying, dying, dying
and longing utterly to die
yet death will not come.

So build your ship of death, and let the soul drift
to dark oblivion.
Maybe life is still our portion
after the bitter passage of oblivion.

All Souls' Day

Be careful, then, and be gentle about death.
For it is hard to die, it is difficult to go through
the door, even when it opens.

And the poor dead, when they have left the walled
and silvery city of the now hopeless body
where are they to go, O where are they to go?

They linger in the shadow of the earth.
The earth's long conical shadow is full of souls
that cannot find the way across the sea of change.

Be kind, Oh be kind to your dead
and give them a little encouragement
and help them to build their little ship of death.

For the soul has a long, long journey after death
to that sweet home of pure oblivion.
Each needs a little ship, a little ship
and the proper store of meal for the longest journey.

Oh, from out of your heart
provide for your dead once more, equip them
like departing mariners, lovingly.

The Houseless Dead

O pity the dead that are dead, but cannot take
the journey, still they moan and beat
against the silvery adamant walls of life's exclusive city.

Oh pity the dead that were ousted out of life
all unequipped to take the long, long voyage.
Gaunt, gaunt they crowd the grey mud-beaches of shadow
that intervene between the final sea
and the white shores of life.

The poor gaunt dead that cannot die
into the distance with receding oars,
but must roam like outcast dogs on the margins of life!
Oh think of them, and encourage them to build
the bark of their deliverance from the dilemma
of non-existence to far oblivion.

Beware the Unhappy Dead!

Beware the unhappy dead thrust out of life
unready, unprepared, unwilling, unable
to continue on the longest journey.

Oh, now as November draws near
the grey, grey reaches of earth's shadow,
the long mean marginal stretches of our existence
are crowded with lost souls, the uneasy dead
that cannot embark on the slinking sea beyond.

Oh, now they moan and throng in anger, and press back
through breaches in the walls of this our by-no-means
    impregnable existence
seeking their old haunts with cold ghostly rage
old haunts, old habitats, old hearths,
old places of sweet life from which they are thrust out
and can but haunt in disembodied rage.

Oh, but beware, beware the angry dead.
Who knows, who knows how much our modern woe
is due to the angry unappeased dead
that were thrust out of life, and now come back at us
malignant, malignant, for we will not succour them.
Oh on this day for the dead, now November is here
set a place for the dead, with a cushion and soft seat
and put a plate, and put a wine-glass out
and serve the best of food, the fondest wine
for your dead, your unseen dead, and with your hearts
speak with them and give them peace and do them honour.

Or else beware their angry presence, now
within your walls, within your very heart.
Oh, they can lay you waste, the angry dead.
Perhaps even now you are suffering from the havoc they make
unknown within your breast and your deadened loins.

After All Saints' Day

Wrapped in the dark-red mantle of warm memories
the little, slender soul sits swiftly down, and takes the oars
and draws away, away, towards dark depths
wafting with warm love from still-living hearts
breathing on his small frail sail, and helping him on
to the fathomless deeps ahead, far, far from the grey shores
of marginal existence.

Song of Death

Sing the song of death, O sing it!
for without the song of death, the song of life
becomes pointless and silly.

Sing then the song of death, and the longest journey
and what the soul takes with him, and what he leaves behind,
and how he enters fold after fold of deepening darkness
for the cosmos even in death is like a dark whorled shell
whose whorls fold round to the core of soundless silence and
    pivotal oblivion
where the soul comes at last, and has utter peace.

Sing then the core of dark and absolute
oblivion where the soul at last is lost
in utter peace.
Sing the song of death, O sing it!

The End, the Beginning

If there were not an utter and absolute dark
of silence and sheer oblivion
at the core of everything,
how terrible the sun would be,
how ghastly it would be to strike a match, and make a light.

But the very sun himself is pivoted
upon a core of pure oblivion,
so is a candle, even as a match.

And if there were not an absolute, utter forgetting
and a ceasing to know, a perfect ceasing to know
and a silent, sheer cessation of all awareness
how terrible life would be!
how terrible it would be to think and know, to have consciousness!

But dipped, once dipped in dark oblivion
the soul has peace, inward and lovely peace.

Sleep

Sleep is the shadow of death, but not only that.
Sleep is a hint of lovely oblivion.
When I am gone, completely lapsed and gone
and healed from all this ache of being.

Sleep and Waking

In sleep I am not, I am gone
I am given up.
And nothing in the world is lovelier than sleep,
dark, dreamless sleep, in deep oblivion!
Nothing in life is quite as good as this.

Yet there is waking from the soundest sleep,
waking, and waking new.

Did you sleep well?
Ah yes, the sleep of God!
The world is created afresh.

Fatigue

My soul has had a long, hard day
she is tired,
she is seeking oblivion.

O, and in the world
there is no place for the soul to find her oblivion
the after darkness of her peace,
for man has killed the silence of the earth
and ravished all the peaceful oblivious places
where the angels used to alight.

Forget

To be able to forget is to be able to yield
to God who dwells in deep oblivion.
Only in sheer oblivion are we with God.
For when we know in full, we have left off knowing.

Know-All

Man knows nothing
till he knows how not-to-know.

And the greatest of teachers will tell you:
The end of all knowledge is oblivion
sweet, dark oblivion, when I cease
even from myself, and am consummated.

Tabernacle

Come, let us build a temple to oblivion
with seven veils, and an innermost
Holy of Holies of sheer oblivion.

And there oblivion dwells, and the silent soul
may sink into god at last, having passed the veils.

But any one who shall ascribe attributes to god or oblivion
let him be cast out, for blasphemy.
For god is a deeper forgetting far than sleep
and all description is a blasphemy.

Temples

Oh, what we want on earth
is centres here and there of silence and forgetting
where we may cease from knowing, and, as far as we know,
may cease from being
in the sweet wholeness of oblivion.

Shadows

And if tonight my soul may find her peace
in sleep, and sink in good oblivion,
and in the morning wake like a new-opened flower
then I have been dipped again in God, and new-created.

And if, as weeks go round, in the dark of the moon
my spirit darkens and goes out, and soft strange gloom
pervades my movements and my thoughts and words
then I shall know that I am walking still
with God, we are close together now the moon's in shadow.

And if, as autumn deepens and darkens
I feel the pain of falling leaves, and stems that break in storms
and trouble and dissolution and distress
and then the softness of deep shadows folding, folding
around my soul and spirit, around my lips
so sweet, like a swoon, or more like the drowse of a low, sad song
singing darker than the nightingale, on, on to the solstice
and the silence of short days, the silence of the year, the shadow,
then I shall know that my life is moving still
with the dark earth, and drenched
with the deep oblivion of earth's lapse and renewal.

And if, in the changing phases of a man's life
I fall in sickness and misery
my wrists seem broken and my heart seems dead
and strength is gone, and my life
is only the leavings of a life:

and still, among it all, snatches of lovely oblivion, and snatches
of renewal
odd, wintry flowers upon the withered stem, yet new, strange
flowers
such as my life has not brought forth before, new blossoms of me—

then I must know that still
I am in the hands of the unknown God,
he is breaking me down to his own oblivion
to send me forth on a new morning, a new man.

Change

Do you think it is easy to change?
Ah, it is very hard to change and be different.
It means passing through the waters of oblivion.

Phoenix

Are you willing to be sponged out, erased, cancelled,
made nothing?
Are you willing to be made nothing?
dipped in oblivion?

If not, you will never really change.

The phoenix renews her youth
only when she is burnt, burnt alive, burnt down
to hot and flocculent ash.
Then the small stirring of a new small bub in the nest
with strands of down like floating ash
Shows that she is renewing her youth like the eagle
Immortal bird.[14]

Notes

[1] Wikipedia; Wikipedia's "Tiryns" entry. Tiryns is a Mycenaean archaeological site in Argolis in the Peloponnese, and the location from which the mythical hero Heracles was said to have performed his Twelve Labors.

[2] Wikipedia; Wikipedia's "Demiurge" entry. In the Platonic, Neopythagorean, Middle Platonic, and Neoplatonic schools of philosophy, the Demiurge is an artisan-like figure responsible for fashioning and maintaining the physical universe. Various schools of Gnostics adopted the term *demiurge*.

[3] Clove Carnation, "Chabaud Mix" (*Dianthus caryophyllus*), are clove-scented double flowers in a wide range of colors: pink, purple, red, white, and yellow.

[4] Anne "Ninon" de l'Enclos (1620–1705), also spelled Ninon de Lenclos and Ninon de Lanclos, was a French author, courtesan, and patron of the arts.

[5] Tyre is an ancient Phoenician port city which, in myth, is known as the birthplace of Europa (who gave Europe its name) and Dido of Carthage (who gave aid to, and fell in love with, Aeneas of Troy). The name means "rock."

[6] Cane-brake, a thicket of cane.

[7] A trumpet-shaped flower, usually deep blue or azure.

[8] Wikipedia; Wikipedia's "Michaelmas" entry. Michaelmas is a Christian festival observed in many Western Christian liturgical calendars on September 29 and on November 8 in the Eastern Christian traditions. In the Christian angelology of some traditions, the Archangel Michael is considered as the greatest of all the angels, being particularly honored for defeating Satan in the war in heaven.

[9] Wikipedia; Wikipedia's "Catabolism" entry. Catabolism is the set of metabolic pathways that breaks down molecules into smaller units that are either oxidized to release energy or used in other anabolic reactions.

[10] Wikipedia; Wikipedia's "Mana (Oceanic cultures)" entry. In Melanesian and Polynesian cultures, *mana* is a supernatural force that permeates the universe. Anyone or anything can have *mana*. They believed it to be a cultivation or possession of energy and power, rather than being a source of power. It is an intentional force.

[11] Wikipedia; Wikipedia's "Anaxagoras" entry. Anaxagoras, "lord of the assembly" (c. 500–c. 428 BC), was a Pre-Socratic Greek philosopher. Responding to the claims of Parmenides on the impossibility of change, Anaxagoras introduced the concept of *Nous* (Cosmic Mind) as an ordering force. He also gave several novel scientific accounts of natural phenomena, including the notion of panspermia, that life exists throughout the universe and could be distributed everywhere. He deduced a correct explanation for eclipses and described the Sun as a fiery mass larger than the Peloponnese, and also attempted to explain rainbows and meteors. He also speculated that the sun might be just another star.

[12] Ithyphallic: of or relating to the phallus carried in procession in ancient festivals of Bacchus.

[13] Theoi.com; Theoi "Attis" entry. Attis was the ancient Phrygian god of vegetation and consort of the great Mother of the Gods Kybele (Cybele). As punishment for his infidelity, the goddess drove him into a mad frenzy, which caused him to castrate himself. Initiates into the eunuch-priesthood of Kybele, known as Gallai (Galli), reenacted this myth with an act of self-castration.

[14] Wikipedia; Wikipedia "Phoenix (mythology)" entry. The phoenixis a legendary immortal bird that cyclically regenerates or is otherwise born again. Originating in Greek mythology, it has analogs in many cultures, such as Egyptian and Persian mythology. Associated with the sun, a phoenix obtains new life by rising from the ashes of its predecessor. Some legends say it dies in a show of flames and combustion, while others say that it simply dies and decomposes before being born again.

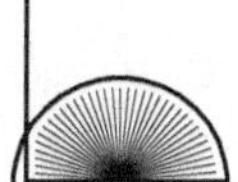

BERGAMOT BOOKS

Bergamot Books publishes books that penetrate the human soul—the realm of feelings, families, and personal experiences through fiction, poetry, memoirs, and spiritual learning. Our books share deeply felt journeys into other places, other lives, and other cultures for readers who are not only curious but also consider themselves world citizens and seekers.

A NOTE ON THE TYPE

The Ship of Death: Last Poems was set in Garamond Premier Pro, designed by Robert Slimbach and developed based on multiple specimens at the Plantin-Moretus Museum in Belgium. It was released by Adobe in 2005.

www.ingramcontent.com/pod-product-compliance
Lightning Source LLC
LaVergne TN
LVHW090534110826
845146LV00003B/1095

* 9 7 9 8 9 9 9 0 1 7 5 0 5 *